anythink

D0722907

Prisms

BY NANCY FURSTINGER

The Child's World

Published by The Child's World®
1980 Lookout Drive • Mankato, MN 56003-1705
800-599-READ • www.childsworld.com

Acknowledgments
The Child's World®: Mary Berendes, Publishing Director
Red Line Editorial: Editorial direction
The Design Lab: Design

Photographs ©: iStockphoto/Thinkstock, cover (bottom left), 1 (bottom left), 11, 13, 17, 21; PhotoDisc, cover (center), 1 (center) 12; A Gorohov/Shutterstock Images, cover (top left), 1 (top left), 3 (right), 16; Shutterstock Images, cover (right), 1 (right), 3 (left), 4, 7, 9, 10, 18, 20, 22; Brand X Pictures/Thinkstock, 14; Ingram Publishing/Thinkstock, 15

ISBN 9781623239848
LCCN 2013947243

Printed in the United States of America
Mankato, MN
November, 2013
PA02194

ABOUT THE AUTHOR

Award-winning author Nancy Furstinger enjoys searching for inspiring shapes in nature as she hikes with her big pooches. She is the author of more than 100 books.

CONTENTS

MAKING RAINBOWS

In science class, the teacher passes out glass prisms. She tells us we can use the three-sided shapes to make rainbows indoors.

We hold our glass prisms up to the sunlight. Against the opposite wall, we can see a rainbow of colors: red, orange, yellow, green, blue, and violet. Our teacher tells us

A glass prism makes rainbows. A prism is also a shape!

that white light is made of many colors. When it passes through the prism, it separates into the colors of the rainbow.

In art class you fold a piece of paper into thirds. You write your name on it and decorate it. Now you have a nameplate for your desk. Did you notice how the shape of the glass prism matches the shape of the nameplate? Both of these shapes are **prisms**.

How Prisms Work

As the white light passes through the glass prism, the light bends. The different colors that make up white light become separated. Coming out of the prism, each color bends at a slightly different angle. Red bends the least. Violet bends the most. That's why the colors separate to create a rainbow effect.

WHAT DOES A PRISM LOOK LIKE?

Prisms are everywhere around us. Prisms are not flat. They have three **dimensions**. Shapes with only two dimensions, like a triangle, are flat. These flat shapes are also called plane shapes or 2-D shapes. They have length and width.

Shapes like prisms that have three dimensions are called **3-D** shapes. Prisms have three dimensions we can measure: length, width, and height. 3-D shapes are also called solid shapes.

How can we identify a prism? Look closely. A prism has a top, bottom, and sides, called **faces**.

These faces are two-dimensional flat **surfaces**. Each face forms a surface of a 3-D shape.

The ends of a prism have two faces that match. Different types of prisms have different shapes. Each prism is named for the shape of its ends, or **base**.

This building is a prism with five sides. Prisms can have three, four, five, or more sides.

A prism's base can be a triangle, a rectangle, or a square. The base can even be a pentagon with five sides, a hexagon with six sides, or an octagon with eight sides. The two bases of a prism are always identical. They are exactly the same shape and size. The bases are **parallel**, too.

The number of sides depends upon the shape of the prism. A triangular prism has three sides. A rectangular prism has four sides. A pentagonal prism has five sides. A hexagonal prism has six sides. An octagonal prism has eight sides.

The base of a prism can come in several shapes. This is a hexagonal prism with six sides.

base →

side

PRISMS AND TRIANGLES

Now that you know what a prism looks like, you can easily find this 3-D shape. You'll start seeing prisms in everyday objects.

It's summertime, and your family hikes along your favorite forest trail. You find the perfect campsite—flat and near the lake. Time to set up your roomy tent. First, pound in your tent stakes. Then assemble the poles. Finally, put up your tent.

You hike past cabins in the woods. These A-frame houses are shaped like a big letter A. This shape allows heavy snow to slide off the roof and down to the ground.

Back home, you set up a tent frame in your bedroom. Cover it with a quilt and fill it with pillows. Now you have a special hideaway to enjoy!

Did you notice all of these places are shaped like triangular prisms? They have bases that are triangles. The other three sides are rectangles.

The roof of this house goes all the way to the ground. It makes a triangular prism.

PRISMS AND RECTANGLES

Today is your teacher's birthday. You bake her a big batch of brownies. Then you carefully layer them in a box. You hope your teacher will share the brownies with your class.

Someone in your class gives your teacher a new lunchbox. Another student brings juice boxes. The juice goes great with the brownies!

These presents are all rectangular prisms.

The principal brings your teacher a dictionary. And after school, the janitor arrives with a box of chalk and a new eraser.

Did you notice that all of the presents are shaped like rectangular prisms? They have two bases and four faces that are all rectangles.

PRISMS AND CUBES

Your little brother cranks the handle of his jack-in-the-box. The song "Pop Goes the Weasel" plays. Suddenly, a clown pops out of the box!

You pull a board game off the shelf. Shake the dice and roll them. Who can race around

the board first? Later, you take out a set of alphabet blocks and help your brother spell words.

Did you know that another 3-D shape is a special type of rectangular prism? This shape is called a cube. The cube has six equal faces. Each face is an identical square. Look closely at your brother's toys. They're all cubes.

Dice are cubes, a special type of prism. All of a cube's sides are the same.

MANY-SIDED PRISMS

When your family stops for a yard sale, you search for prisms. That crystal paperweight could be a prism. You closely examine it. The paperweight has five sides, so it's a pentagonal prism.

This jewelry box has six sides. It is a hexagonal prism.

Next, you find a box of yellow pencils. Take a new pencil out of the box and count its sides.

There are six, so
the pencil is a
hexagonal prism.
You spot a
splendid music
box. When you
open the lid,
a song starts
playing. This
box looks old
and beautiful. As you bring the box
to your mother, count the sides. There
are eight, so the box is an octagonal prism.

Can you find the hexagonal prism in this scene? Do you see any other prisms?

BEES AND PRISMS

Smart bees build their honeycombs using prisms that have six sides. Look closely at a honeycomb. Every cell is shaped like a hexagon. All of these shapes fit together like a jigsaw puzzle.

The cells in a bee's honeycomb are hexagonal prisms.

Have you ever wondered why bees use this shape? The hexagon requires less beeswax to build than other shapes. Keep in mind that it takes eight ounces of honey to make one ounce of beeswax. With a hexagon shape, bees don't have to work as hard.

And when the honeycomb is finished, it holds more honey than if the bees used other shapes. No wonder a hive full of honey is so heavy!

Copying the Honeycomb Design

People often look to nature for ideas. When inventors realized how smart the honeycomb shape is, they got to work. Now there are new products using this strong and lightweight hexagon. Honeycomb panels are sandwiched between two pieces of metal. Then this material is used in airplanes, trains, and buildings.

CRYSTAL PRISMS AND GIANT PRISMS

You can find more prism shapes in nature. Sometimes crystals and rocks form prism shapes.

Garnets are beautiful gems. They come in almost every color of the rainbow, especially reds and greens. The garnet is the state gemstone of New York. Many garnets form as prisms.

Garnets often form as cubes or rectangular prisms.

Some rocks are huge prisms. The Giant's Causeway is in Northern Ireland. These pillars of stone are made from basalt rock. But an ancient story says they formed in a fight between two giants!

Search for prism shapes in your house and everywhere you go. You'll be amazed how many of these 3-D shapes you can find!

The stones of the Giant's Causeway are shaped like prisms.

HANDS-ON ACTIVITY: PRISM POSTERS

Use this poster to display different shaped prisms. You could even bring your poster to show-and-tell!

Materials

- magazines
- poster board
- scissors
- glue stick
- markers

Directions

1. Search in magazines for real-life examples of prisms. Cut out the photographs that you find.
2. Arrange the photographs by what type of base the prism has. Remember, prisms can have a base that is a triangle, rectangle, square, pentagon, hexagon, or octagon.
3. When you're happy with your arrangement, glue the photographs to the poster board. Let the glue dry.
4. Write captions telling what type of prism your photographs show. Display your poster.

GLOSSARY

base (BASE): A base is a flat surface on a 3-D shape. A prism is named for the shape of its base.

dimensions (duh-MEN-shuns): Dimensions are the length, width, or height of an object. A prism's height is one of its dimensions.

faces (FASE-uhs): Faces are flat surfaces on a 3-D shape. A prism has several faces.

parallel (PAYR-uh-lel): Lines that are parallel are always the same distance apart. Parallel lines never meet.

prisms (PRIZ-uhms): Prisms are 3-D shapes with bases that are identical shapes and sides that are parallel. Honeycombs and boxes are two examples of prisms.

surfaces (SUR-fas-uhs): Surfaces are the flat or curved borders of a 3-D shape. A prism has several flat surfaces.

3-D (THREE-DEE): A 3-D shape has three dimensions: length, width, and height. A 3-D shape is not flat.

BOOKS

Anderson, Moira. *Shapes in Our World*. Huntington Beach, CA: Teacher Created Materials Publishing, 2009.

Cohen, Marina. *My Path to Math: 3-D Shapes*. New York: Crabtree Publishing Company, 2011.

WEB SITES

Visit our Web site for links about Prisms: *childsworld.com/links*

Note to Parents, Teachers, and Librarians:
We routinely verify our Web links to make sure they are safe and active sites. So encourage your readers to check them out!

INDEX